Pebble® Plus Pet Questions and Answers

HAMSTERS

Questions and Answers

by Christina Mia Gardeski

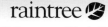
raintree

a Capstone company — publishers for children

Raintree is an imprint of Capstone Global Library Limited, a company incorporated in England and Wales having its registered office at 264 Banbury Road, Oxford, OX2 7DY – Registered company number: 6695582

www.raintree.co.uk
myorders@raintree.co.uk

Edited by Carrie Braulick Sheely and Michelle Hasselius
Designed by Kayla Rossow
Picture research by Pam Mitsakos
Production by Gene Bentdahl

ISBN 978 1 4747 2139 4
20 19 18 17 16
10 9 8 7 6 5 4 3 2 1

British Library Cataloguing in Publication Data
A full catalogue record for this book is available from the British Library.

Every effort has been made to contact copyright holders of material reproduced in this book. Any omissions will be rectified in subsequent printings if notice is given to the publisher.

All the internet addresses (URLs) given in this book were valid at the time of going to press. However, due to the dynamic nature of the internet, some addresses may have changed, or sites may have changed or ceased to exist since publication. While the author and publisher regret any inconvenience this may cause readers, no responsibility for any such changes can be accepted by either the author or the publisher.

Acknowledgements
Alamy: imageBROKER, 19, Juniors Bildarchiv GmbH, 5; Dreamstime: Alexkalashnikov, 11; iStockphoto: snapphoto, 17; Shutterstock: AlexKalashnikov, 7, cover, DoubleBubble, 1, 22, Jane September, 21, Steve Design, 13, stock_shot, 15; Thinkstock: DimitrovoPhtography, 9

Printed and bound in China.

Contents

Who has a mouthful?

My hamster!

Hamsters keep food in

big pouches in their cheeks.

They do not eat the food all

at once. They save it for later.

Why is my hamster up at night?

Hamsters sleep during the day. They have lots of energy at night. They chew on toys and spin hamster wheels. Your noisy friend might keep you awake!

Can hamsters see in the dark?

Hamsters cannot see well. They can see less than 15 centimetres in front of their noses. They use their whiskers to feel what is around them.

Where can I keep my hamster?

Most pet hamsters live alone in a

big cage. Add deep bedding,

a hamster wheel and toy tunnels.

Keep the cage away from

hot and cold places and other pets.

What do hamsters eat?

Pet hamsters eat dry pellets of food. They can also eat a mixture of seeds, grains and nuts. They like fruit and vegetables. They drink fresh water from a hanging bottle.

Why do hamsters dig?

Wild hamsters live in burrows

they dig under ground.

Pet hamsters dig in their bedding.

They hide food there.

Can I let my hamster out of its cage?

A free hamster can get lost. Let your hamster run inside a hamster ball away from stairs. Always watch your hamster closely when he is outside of the cage.

Can my hamster catch my cold?

Hamsters can get colds from people.

Try not to sneeze or cough

near your hamster.

Wash your hands before

touching it or its food.

How long do hamsters live for?

Hamsters can live for up to three years. Their small bodies can be hurt easily. Be gentle when you play with your hamster.

Glossary

bedding soft, shredded wood, paper or other material that can be used for an animal's bed

burrow tunnel or hole in the ground made or used by an animal

energy strength to do active things without getting tired

hamster ball empty ball that a hamster can go inside to run

pellet small, dry piece of hamster food

pouch large space in a hamster's cheek used to store food

whisker one of the long hairs growing on the face and bodies of some animals

Read more

Care for your Hamster (RSPCA Pet Guide), RSPCA (HarperCollins, 2015)

Looking After Hamsters (Usborne Pet Guides), Susan Meredith (Usborne Publishing Ltd, 2013)

Nibble's Guide to Caring for Your Hamster (Pets' Guides), Anita Ganeri (Raintree, 2014)

Websites

www.dkfindout.com/uk/animals-and-nature/pet-care
Find out more about pet care.

www.rspca.org.uk/adviceandwelfare/pets/rodents/hamsters
Find out more about owning a hamster.

Comprehension questions

1. Hamsters use their whiskers to feel what is around them. What are whiskers?

2. Why do hamsters dig?

3. How can you try to make sure your hamster doesn't catch your cold?

Index